Delhi Thaatha

Delhi Thaatha

A GREAT GRAND STORY

CHITRA VIRARAGHAVAN

ILLUSTRATED BY SUNANDINI BANERJEE

WITH SKETCHES BY P. BALASUBRAMANIAN

LONDON NEW YORK CALCUTTA

Seagull Books, 2018

Text © Chitra Viraraghavan, 2018
Digital collages © Sunandini Banerjee, 2018
Photographs and paintings © Individual photographers and artists

ISBN 978 0 8574 2 549 2

British Library Cataloguing-in-Publication Data
A catalogue record for this book is available from the British Library

Designed by Sunandini Banerjee, Seagull Books, Calcutta, India
Printed and bound by Hyam Enterprises, Calcutta, India

In memory of
Sundari
and her siblings

and for
Indira

I call him Delhi Thaatha.

But he lives in Madras. And he isn't my grandfather.

He's my great-grandfather.

Here is his house.

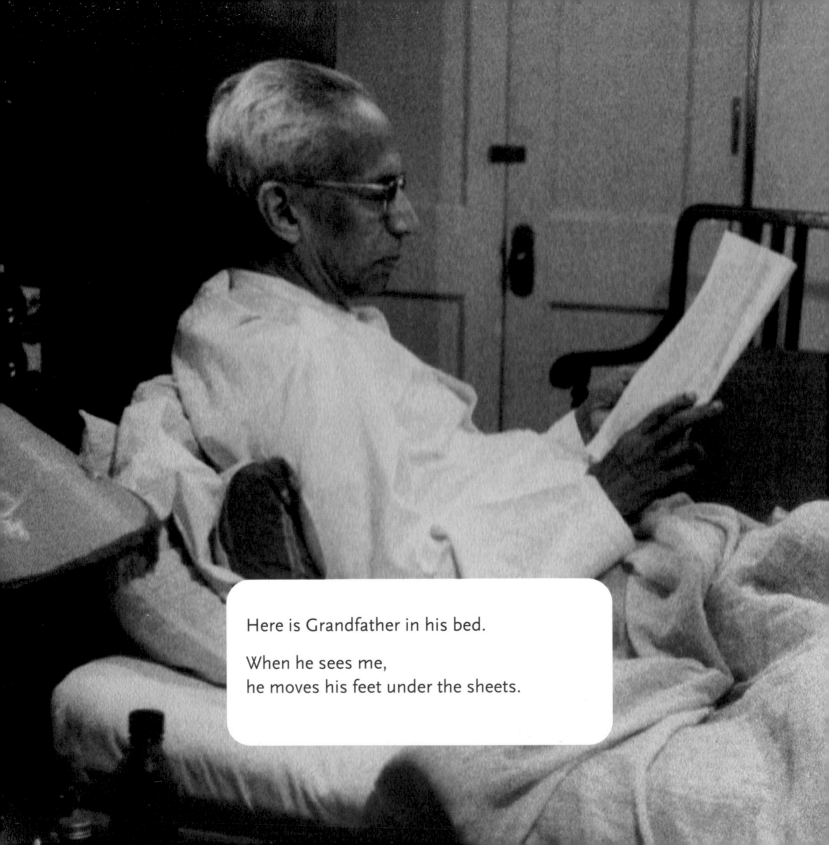

Here is Grandfather in his bed.

When he sees me,
he moves his feet under the sheets.

4 5 6 7

But I'm SEVEN years old.

I know better.

Grandfather didn't always live in this house.

He grew up in a very small town.

It looked something like this.

Every day, Grandfather set off to school.

His mother would give him a bag of peanuts for lunch.

One day, a thief caught the boy. 'Hand me your gold or I'll throw you down this well!' he said. But all he found was the bag of peanuts. The man grabbed the peanuts.

Grandfather didn't mind.

He knew there were people who had nothing to eat at all.

Grandfather was a naughty boy. He found school very easy. So sometimes he stayed away.

He walked around for miles and miles. He walked through forests and fields and villages.

He followed railway tracks to see where they went.

He looked and listened and thought about things.

His mother and father found out that he was skipping school. So they sent him to school in another town.

When it was time for him to go to college, his parents counted all the money they had. It was just enough to send him there.

But he had no money to buy books. So he used his cousin's.

Grandfather read his books every night by the light of a lantern. He thought about things some more.

'What did you think about, Thaatha?'

'I thought about feelings,' he said.

'Like when you are hungry or angry?' I said.

'Yes. And when you are happy or sad,' he said.

I remembered how happy I was when I got Curly for my birthday.

Here is a picture of Curly.

'What else did you think about, Thaatha?'

'I thought if we know what we feel it is easy to be happy.'

I thought about how I felt when my best friend went away.

'But I felt sad when Mona left, Thaatha!'

'But won't Mona always be your friend?' he said, smoothing my hair.

I thought for a bit. 'Yes, she will.'

'So then she'll always be a part of you, won't she?'

'Yes . . . ' I said, not sure.

'Of course she will!' he said, smiling. 'So that should make you happy!'

Grandfather was good at explaining things. That's why he became a teacher.

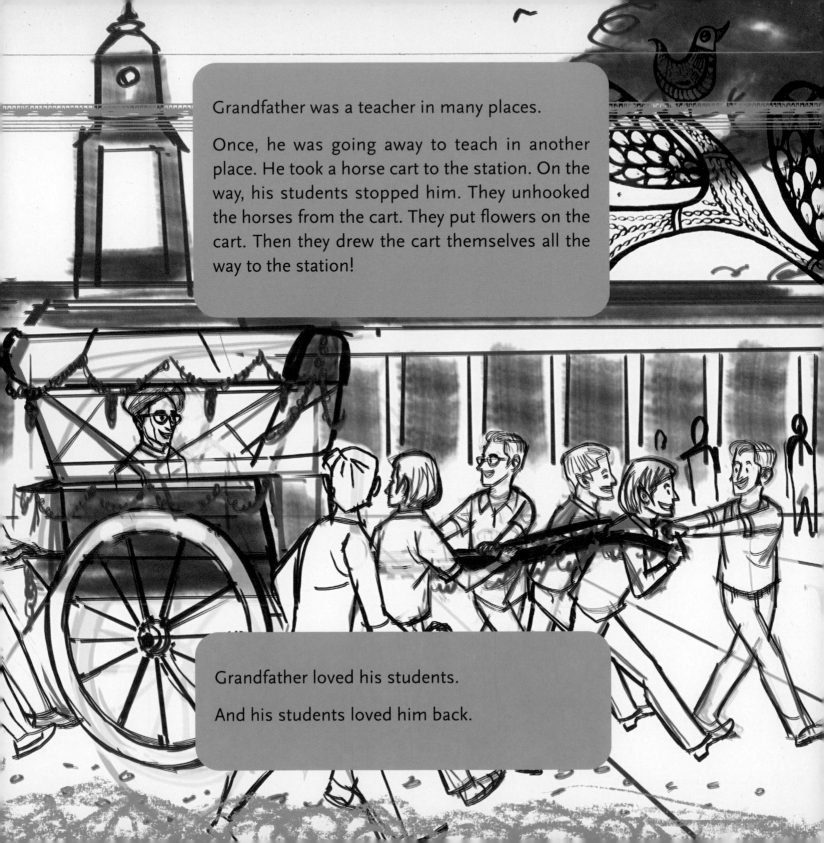

Grandfather was a teacher in many places.

Once, he was going away to teach in another place. He took a horse cart to the station. On the way, his students stopped him. They unhooked the horses from the cart. They put flowers on the cart. Then they drew the cart themselves all the way to the station!

Grandfather loved his students.

And his students loved him back.

RECOVERY OF FAITH

An Idealist View of Life

The Principal Upanishads

Eastern Religions and Western Thought

The Philosophy of Rabindranath Tagore

Grandfather wrote books to explain things. Here are some of them. They have long words.

Grandfather says long words are easy. All you do is break them up. Like phi – los – o – phy. See?

People liked what Grandfather said in his books. They asked him to come and speak to them. And so he did.

Grandfather went to many places. He went to Calcutta and Oxford. He went to Banaras and Moscow. Look at them on this map.

In Moscow, Grandfather met someone called Mr Stalin. Mr Stalin was a scary man. People were afraid of him.

When it was time for Grandfather to go back home to India, he visited Mr Stalin to say good-bye. Mr Stalin was old and not very well.

As Grandfather was leaving, Mr Stalin came around his desk to shake his hand.

Grandfather patted Mr Stalin on his cheek. 'Look after yourself,' he said.

Mr Stalin was happy. 'No one has been so kind to me,' he said.

But Grandfather is kind to everyone. He has the twinkliest eyes ever! Twink – li – est. Is that a word? No, I just made it up!

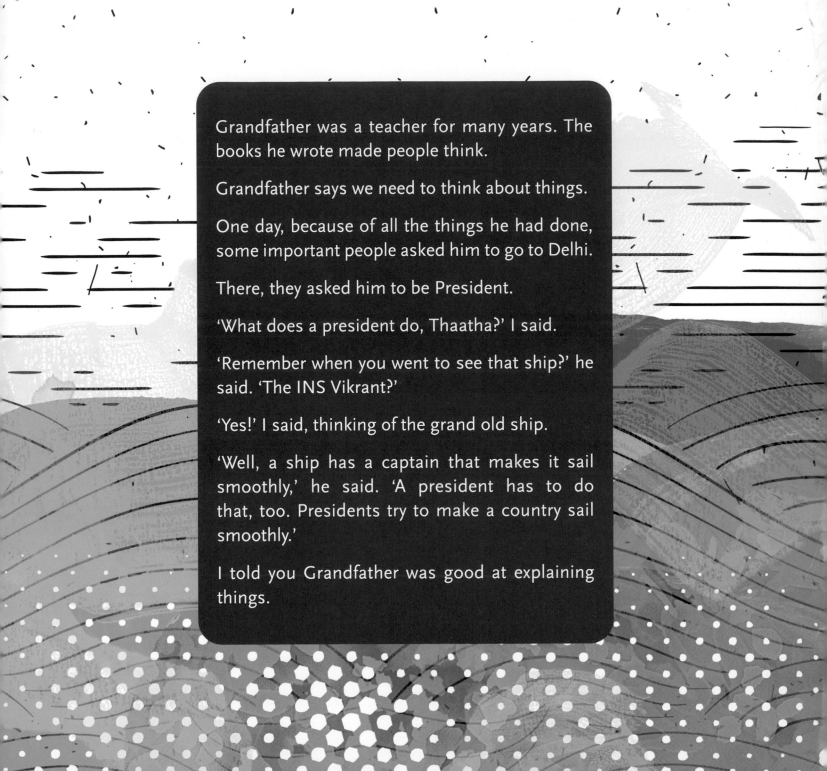

Grandfather was a teacher for many years. The books he wrote made people think.

Grandfather says we need to think about things.

One day, because of all the things he had done, some important people asked him to go to Delhi.

There, they asked him to be President.

'What does a president do, Thaatha?' I said.

'Remember when you went to see that ship?' he said. 'The INS Vikrant?'

'Yes!' I said, thinking of the grand old ship.

'Well, a ship has a captain that makes it sail smoothly,' he said. 'A president has to do that, too. Presidents try to make a country sail smoothly.'

I told you Grandfather was good at explaining things.

In Delhi, he lived in this house.

Grandfather lived in Delhi for some time. That's why I call him Delhi Thaatha.

After a few years, he came home to Madras to live.

Grandfather lay on his bed reading.

'What are you doing, dear?' he said, looking at me over his glasses.

'Writing a story, Thaatha,' I said.

The End

A Note from the Author

Sarvepalli Radhakrishnan was my maternal great-grandfather: the father of Sundari, my mother's mother. Not everyone gets to spend time they remember with a great-grandparent; I was lucky not just in this, but in the kind of person he was.

This book is based on fact, memory, family lore and reminiscence. The memories include my own of my great-grandfather; the family lore and reminiscences I owe to my grandmother, great-aunt and mother; the facts, in the main, to my great-uncle's biography of his father. Some of the conversations with my great-granddad were real; others I conjured up, always keeping in mind the facts. I could tell you as children's writer that this seemed a more dramatic way of giving young readers a sense of my subject and his personality. But the truth is this: both text and structure came unbidden, in two days flat, some forty years after, automatically weaving together details of my great-grandfather's life with some from my own.

I owe thanks to many in my family: the late Sundari Sandilya, for stories from her father's life; the late Sarvepalli Gopal for *Radhakrishnan: A Biography*; Indira Gopal, for allowing me to see her father-in-law through the dual lenses of her great devotion and deep affection; Girija Viraraghavan, for insight into her grandfather's personality, and for making sure my brother, Vijay, and I spent time with him whenever we were in Madras; Keshav Desiraju, for helping me locate and sort out photographs of our mutual ancestor from the family albums; M. S. Viraraghavan, for his unwavering faith in me and my projects, however whimsical; my parents, both for their implicit belief in not basking in referred light but in finding one's own; and Krishna Shastri Devulapalli, collaborator in all projects, creative or otherwise.

I also owe thanks to my friend Vani Vasudevan, with kindly editorial eye and vast experience in children's books, for first endorsing both text and me; to friend, and first editor, Karthika V. K., for introducing me to Seagull Books; to the wonderful Sunandini Banerjee of Seagull Books for so very graciously agreeing to illuminate this book, thereby extending the narrative in her own extraordinary way; my artist friend P. Balasubramanian, for the lively and affectionate sketches of Thaatha and me found in various parts of the book, as also the evocative carriage scene; and to the ever independent-minded Naveen Kishore of Seagull Books, for his warm, generous and spontaneous backing of a difficult-to-classify book at which other publishers may have baulked.

I hope that Sundari and her siblings Padmavathi, Rukmini, Sushila, Shakuntala and Gopal would have been happy with this little book on their father.

Acknowledgements

The many unidentifiable photographers from India and elsewhere, for photographs of Sarvepalli Radhakrishnan, sourced from the family's personal collection. The late T. S. Satyan, for photographs of Radhakrishnan presented to the family. Sundar Natarajan, for the photograph of Radhakrishnan's house in Madras.

Chandana Hore, for the painting by Somnath Hore, used here to represent a thoughtful young Radhakrishnan.

Manasij Dutta of Seagull Books for his gentle illustration of the tiny town of Tirutanni as it may have once looked, of Madras Christian College and of Joseph Stalin.

Alice Attie, for the use of her sketches across many of the collages.